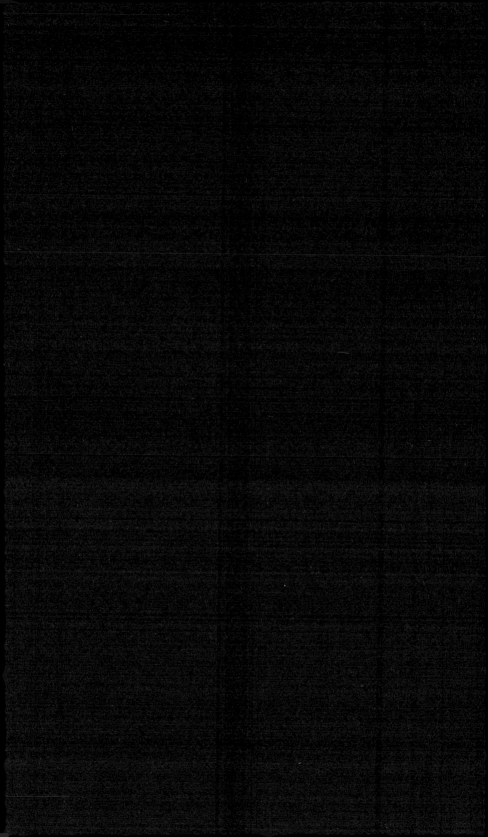

OVERTIME

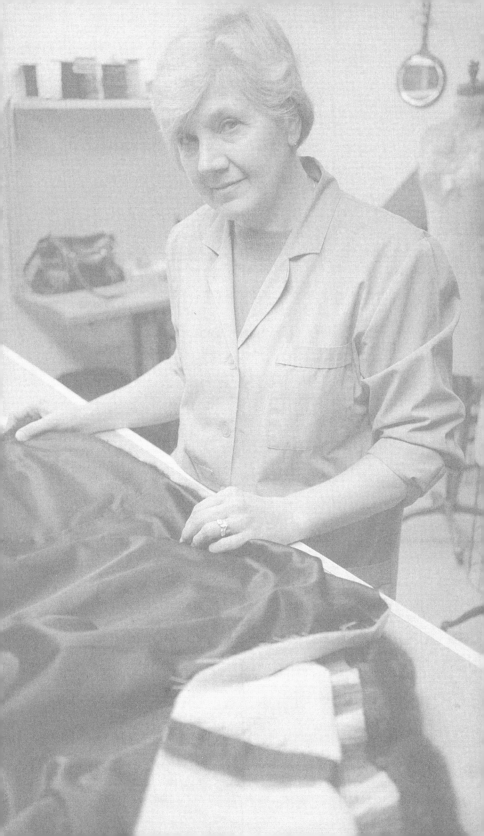

Portraits of a Vanishing Canada

OVERTIME

Karl Kessler & Sunshine Chen

with a Foreword by Nora Young

The Porcupine's Quill

Library and Archives Canada Cataloguing in Publication

Kessler, Karl, 1970–, author
     Overtime : portraits of a vanishing Canada / Karl Kessler & Sunshine Chen ;
with a foreword by Nora Young.

ISBN 978-0-88984-415-5 (softcover)

     1. Professional employees—Ontario—Waterloo Region—Pictorial works.
2. Professional employees—Ontario—Waterloo Region—Interviews. 3. Building
trades—Ontario—Waterloo Region—Employees—Pictorial works. 4. Building
trades—Ontario—Waterloo Region—Employees—Interviews. 5. Artisans—
Ontario—Waterloo Region—Pictorial works. 6. Artisans—Ontario—Waterloo
Region—Interviews. 7. Professions—Ontario—Waterloo Region. I. Chen,
Sunshine, 1972–, author II. Title.

HD8038.C22W38 2018   331.7'10971345   C2018-904507-8

Published by The Porcupine's Quill, 68 Main Street, PO Box 160,
Erin, Ontario NOB 1TO. http://porcupinesquill.ca

Readied for the press by Stephanie Small. Represented in Canada by Canadian
Manda. Trade orders are available from University of Toronto Press.

We acknowledge the support of the Ontario Arts Council and the Canada Council
for the Arts for our publishing program. The financial support of the Government
of Canada is also gratefully acknowledged.

Canada Council Conseil des arts
for the Arts   du Canada

ONTARIO ARTS COUNCIL
CONSEIL DES ARTS DE L'ONTARIO
an Ontario government agency
un organisme du gouvernement de l'Ontario

Canadä

Ontario
Ontario Media Development
Corporation

For Harvey Wang of New York.
For Jack and Tom Dolly, the best bosses in town.
For Dad, for enduring.

Karl Kessler

∾

For all the honest, hardworking people who shared
their stories of life and love, and of getting by.
For my parents, who got by, so that we could flourish.

Sunshine Chen

☞ Most of the time, we don't think a lot about our tools and technologies, or about how we use them. The things we use every day—ovens, bicycles, pens—don't even seem to us like technologies at all, though of course they are.

In our current time of digital transformation, we ask all kinds of questions about our new technologies: how they should be designed, what rules should govern them, is it okay to text someone while you're talking to the person in front of you (no). The questions we ask about our use of social networks, for example, range from individual etiquette all the way to how we regulate these platforms so they don't subvert our democracy.

This is because it's all so new, we're aware that things could be different. Technology is part of culture, and when technology changes, so too must the culture.

What we do less often in these moments of great technological change is look at the technology and culture that are waning. If we do, it's with a sort of whimsy or nostalgia. We think fondly about what it was like to get a letter in the mail from a faraway friend, or we chuckle about what it was like listening to eight-track tapes in the car.

A project like this, though, is an invitation to reflect in a way that's deeper and more satisfying than nostalgia. In seeing these images and reading about people's life's work, we see how much of our culture—our very way of being in the world—is expressed in the work we do, and the tools we use to do that work.

Through these images and profiles, we see how the jobs we have and the tools we use to carry them out are tightly linked. We know, of course, that our work is a big part of what gives our lives a narrative arc, giving shape to our days and a feeling of purpose. But it's hard to talk about our jobs having meaning for us, as part of the total of what gives our lives meaning, without calling to mind the things we use to accomplish that work. We have a kind of intimate relationship with our tools. That's true whether we work on a computer, or make brooms the way they were made long ago.

And yet, though that's true of all our tools and jobs, there's something, I think, about the physicality and tactility of the skills depicted here which points to what is gained and lost in the growing transition from analog to digital. In my own life, I can still recall the feeling of editing audio on reel-to-reel tape using razor blades and wax pencils, although it's something I only did very briefly before the move to digital. It's hard to imagine having that same 'body memory' of pressing 'control x' on a keyboard.

There's a reason why vinyl albums sales are growing, for example, alongside streaming music services, even amongst young people who didn't grow up with the technology. This is not sentimentality or nostalgia. It's a deeply human connection to tactility, to the here-and-nowness of things.

Beyond the personal, looking at skills, jobs, and whole industries in decline shows us something at a bigger level. It's an opportunity to reflect on things like scale, and speed, and most significantly, our sense of place.

Today's digital industry puts the priority on 'scalability' in a truly novel way. Such is the virtual nature of zeroes and ones that we can talk, astonishingly, about global corporations that scale to billions of users, sending data all around the planet. It's easy to forget that these global companies were born in particular cultures and economies themselves, and that, as numerous critics have pointed out, they tend to express the values and biases of Silicon Valley.

So we live in a time that hasn't transcended place, but rather tends to conceal it. Our sense of time is also altered. We are growing used to things that happen apparently instantly. When there is a hiccup, and our digital media don't work immediately, we're irrationally infuriated, staring blankly at our dead screens. And yet, alongside this, we look for opportunities to slow down, to unplug, to experience the unfolding of time. We seem to crave it.

Through the long lens of history, the impact of technological change on culture and society is startlingly obvious. Famously, the revolution brought on by Gutenberg and the spread of the printing press is credited with all kinds of cultural changes, from the growth of literacy to the 'invention' of the private individual. It's hard to discern these changes when we're in the midst of them, but looking to the near past, as well as the near future, helps us see how the shape of our lives, and our culture, are changing.

Nora Young
Toronto, 2018

Introduction

☞ Things change, in every age, every place. As they must.

Neighbourhoods turn over, and then over again. Methods evolve. Materials phase in and out. A leading-edge technology emerges like a wave and what once was state-of-the-art slips behind the crest, to the trailing edge, hidden by the new.

People change too. Even those who seem frozen in time move forward with the rest, as also they must, but on the back of the wave, riding the trailing edge. They adapt, and carry on. In the short term, the obsolete is their stock-in-trade, and arcane knowledge is their currency. But over the long run—theirs longer than most—their point of view is panoramic.

Begun in 2008, *Overtime* is a record of fifty people practising trades, professions and cultural traditions in decline in the early years of the new century. A few of these practices had always been uncommon. Most of the rest were once widespread. For some it was a slow fade, for others a vanishing act. For each, an environmental portrait photograph is paired with a short written profile based on an interview.

The participants were located in the three cities and four townships of Ontario's Waterloo Region, but together they are a microcosm: across the province and beyond, technological, economic and societal changes have meant an end to many long-established trades and customs that were ingrained in the twentieth-century experience. Traditional manufacturing has been deeply affected by automation and global trade. Web-based commerce, changing consumer habits and rising Main Street rents have made independent storefront retail a perilous enterprise. An entire working life spent in the same profession, or employed by the same company, is no longer the common thing it was, and it's now rare for a family to ply the same trade over successive generations.

The people in this book have swum against these currents. And yet stories such as theirs are seldom brought to light, except perhaps when a store announces its closeout sale, an organization folds, a factory is slated for shutdown. In Waterloo Region, this is in spite of an expanding tech sector and a recent building boom that stand in sharp contrast to these kinds of changes.

While we laud the new, the whos and the whats slipping behind the wave, if considered at all, have often been an afterthought. This book is offered in forethought.

The next breakthrough will herald another obsolescence, and to the passing of time we may concede a tool or a trade, a tradition or an era, but no person ever is obsolete, as those who follow here will attest.

༄

Overtime takes its inspiration from *Harvey Wang's New York* by Harvey Wang, published in 1990, so good it holds out against time.

Sunshine Chen conducted and recorded each *Overtime* interview, on-site, the same day as the photo shoot. I did the photography and writing.

In keeping with the spirit of our project, I made the photographs on medium-format black-and-white film.

The profile texts are in the present tense to preserve the voices and circumstances of the participants at the time of our visits. Some have since retired, some workplaces have closed, some traditions have ended. A few of the people are no longer living, and their inclusion here is dedicated to their memory.

Karl Kessler
Waterloo, 2018

THE PORTRAITS

Dan Bergeron, Sign Painter

It's always been in me—since I was born, I've been drawing and sketching. When I was a little kid, the teachers used to get me to come up to the blackboard and draw…

⟫ Many years later, the car dealership where Dan Bergeron worked needed a sign. He volunteered to paint it. Next he lettered the windows. Soon he had left the dealership to paint signs full-time. 'I started asking people what kind of paints they used, what kind of brushes, and you'd think you were asking for their firstborn. They wouldn't tell you anything.'

Dan's script and show-card-style lettering reveal the skill of an expert: relaxed but controlled, with consistent weight, spacing and slant (the key, Dan says, is to have the right brush). Shadows and highlights, properly placed, make the letters 'pop'.

As cut-vinyl lettering replaced paint as the trade standard, Dan stuck with the old standby, Sign Painters' 1 Shot lettering enamel. 'When I started, everybody painted,' Dan says, but now all the sign painters he once knew have packed their brushes away. 'Nobody paints. Some of them are still in business, but they've got a computer. And I went that route when it first became popular, but I found it took all the fun out of my work. I just sat there and listened to the machine cut out my letters.'

Dan once lettered trucks and panel signs, but now he works mainly on store windows, year-round, anywhere in Southwestern Ontario. 'It keeps me hopping. There's not enough of me around! And I'm almost sixty years old, so when somebody comes up to me and asks me, "What kind of brushes do you have?" or "What kind of paint do you use?" I always ask them, "Are you artistic?" If they say "Yeah," I tell them, "This is the paint, that's the brushes, that's where you get them", and I hand them my business card and say, "If you have any questions at all, you call me", because I remember how hard it was for me, breaking into this business.'

Breakfast
EGGS BENNY
BELGIAN WAFFLES
VILLAGE MELTS
OMELETTES
. . . and more !!
Try our "Inc
WINTRIP
ACCOUNTANT
LEASE

John Rumpel, Felt Manufacturer

I don't believe in retirement. Not in a family business. I enjoy it. I don't feel it's work ...

🖝 At the Rumpel Felt Company in early 2008, signs of longevity are everywhere. Through a grand entrance portico and then up a long flight of stairs, a reception window reads ENQUIRY in formal gold-painted lettering. On a wall just beyond hangs a big, old city map and an even bigger, older portrait of company founder George Rumpel. At the back, at a desk in a modest office behind glass-and-oak partitions, sits John Rumpel, George's ninety-two-year-old grandson.

John got into the business when he was a kid. 'The first job I remember, I was still going to school—those days we used to work Saturday, and we used to press the coloured felt, and I ran the press.' He took over management when he was still in his twenties, and his son David is now the fourth generation to run the family business.

Beginning in the nineteenth century, George Rumpel and other entrepreneurs built their factories along Victoria Street and the railway tracks that run next to it, building Kitchener's industrial reputation along with the bricks and mortar. When the local felt industry was at its height, the versatile material was used in products including automotive components, footwear and clothing. Rumpel Felt supplied finished-goods manufacturers locally and across Canada.

But in the first decade of the twenty-first century, a strong Canadian dollar and competition from abroad have hurt many Ontario manufacturers. Work orders have ebbed. Long-running businesses whose employees numbered in the hundreds have closed their doors, and Rumpel Felt, among the oldest still running, is also winding down. 'What killed us is we had no protection government-wise,' says John, 'and offshore businesses pretty well killed the business.' But he has learned to ride the ups and downs—a surging dollar, for example, which he says is 'good and bad: good for a lot of people, and bad for others. But that's life. You can't win 'em all.'

Alf Hannenberg, Felt Worker

I got my first paycheque on my eighteenth birthday. I grossed eighty-three bucks …

☞ Alf Hannenberg started at the Rumpel Felt Company operating the felt-drying equipment, and is finishing his career at Rumpel on the old steam-driven felt presser. 'This is the last machine in the factory that's using steam,' he says, shouting above the noise.

He loads big rolls of felt onto the presser, and as the material feeds through the calender rollers he uses a micrometer to test its thickness, making adjustments when necessary. The process has changed little in a hundred years.

Elsewhere in the factory much of the felt-making machinery has been removed, especially the wet-felting equipment, but the sprawling 'needle-punch' felting machines are still in place, turning cartloads of wool and synthetic fibre into thick, dense material—and making a racket.

Alf has worked all over the plant, in each of the different stages of felt making. His parents met at Rumpel, and his father retired after forty years with the company. His uncle, brother and son also worked here. He remembers when there were about a hundred employees. Now, in early 2008, just weeks before the fourth-generation family-owned company is set to close, there are about a dozen.

Alf says he has been planning for the future, but adds, 'You know, when you're here thirty-seven years you're supposed to retire, not look for another job.... It was my second home.'

Kelly Droppo, Garment Factory Manager

Nobody worried about getting a job. You could quit one and walk down the street and get hired at another place. There was Kaufman Footwear, there was Cline's, there was Arrow, and then Forsyth, all in one little area. People that you'd meet at work usually had worked at all four of them!

🐟 Kelly Droppo got her start in the garment industry when factory work was not hard to find and job hunters could afford to be choosy. 'When I went to high school I wanted to make some extra money. So the John Forsyth Shirt Company that used to be located in downtown Kitchener, they had an afternoon shift.... I sewed pockets on shirts.'

Kelly soon learned all the different sewing jobs at Forsyth. Then she started training new employees, and went on to supervise one department after another. 'Then after that the whole production floor was turned over to me,' she says.

Forsyth eventually moved to Cambridge. It shut down in 2013, but a few months later some former employees, including Kelly, founded a new company, Canadian-Made Apparel, and brought the place back to life. They rehired half of the workers and reactivated the equipment, and orders for shirts and pants started coming in again. 'It seemed almost impossible at the time, but the options, there weren't really any anyway, so there was nothing to lose to go ahead and try. It took us about two weeks,' says Kelly.

The factory is a leaner operation than it once was, but it hums with activity. A fugue of machines and voices blends with pop music from a radio. Shirt fronts, backs, sleeves, collars and cuffs are cut from the cloth and finished in specialized areas on the sewing floor. Then the shirts are assembled, inspected and packaged. Kelly knows all of the steps intuitively. She makes her rounds, talking with the workers, checking equipment, troubleshooting, offering advice. She says having fewer employees means heavier workloads for everyone, but 'the other option is not to have a job at all.'

Mangaria Boodram, Garment Worker

Back home we always sewed. At that time you didn't have clothes that you can go to the store and buy, you just buy the material and then your mom sews, and then you learn from her. Eventually you sew all your dresses, and everything...

✒ As a girl in Guyana, Mangaria 'Asha' Boodram started sewing as soon as she could thread a needle. Since 1984 she has worked as a sewing-machine operator, first at Penmans in Cambridge, then at the John Forsyth Shirt Company, founded in Kitchener in the early 1900s.

The local garment industry was established in the nineteenth century, but when Forsyth closed in 2013 after trade policies made it more difficult for Canadian-based clothing manufacturers to remain competitive, it appeared the end of an era was at hand. Then, within months of the closure, the former plant manager, with help from a few other out-of-work Forsyth employees, created a new company, Canadian-Made Apparel. They restarted the Cambridge factory and hired back many of the workers. The overall direction of the domestic garment industry has been just the opposite: in a marketplace glutted with low-cost clothing made abroad by workers earning comparatively lower wages, many Canadian clothing manufacturers have either moved out of the country or shut down entirely. Asha says this is a lost opportunity. 'A good-quality shirt is made in Canada. We can do the same thing they do overseas. There's good workers in Canada,' she says. 'I notice Penmans labels, but there's no more Penmans in Cambridge. Where is this label coming from? Somewhere else.'

Many days Asha works on uniforms for Canadian retail chains. Today she is sewing shirt yokes. In years past she made a lot of dress shirts—'Beautiful dress shirts, but I don't know where they all went. Probably China...Mexico....'

Asha takes pride in her work, and in her daily travels she keeps her eyes open for shirts she had a hand in making. 'When you see the finished product, you say, "Wow—we made that!"'

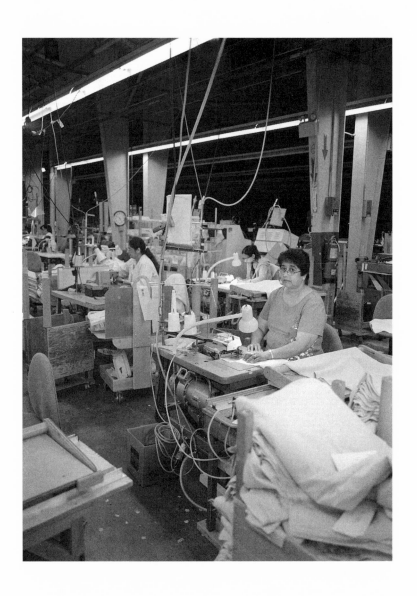

Ken Metzger, Glove Cutter

That's why you have to come in and work at night ...

☞ A tremendous bang and rumble shakes the floor at the Dotzert Glove Company each time Ken Metzger deploys the machine he calls 'the clicker', a vintage Bata hydraulic swing-arm press he uses to die-cut deerskin work gloves. There is a retail store downstairs, so he works after hours. 'When we first started, we worked with the mallets,' Ken says, although now he uses the clicker more than the old mallets and handheld cutting dies. (He demonstrates cutting with a mallet—it's only slightly quieter than the clicker.) Cutting a half-glove cleanly from a hide with a single mallet strike is tricky, but he says it can be done, 'if you're good'. Ken used to work all day with a heavy mallet in one hand and a die in the other, cutting a few dozen gloves per hour. 'The machine does not necessarily mean it's faster than cutting it by hand,' he says. 'Sometimes it can be slower. But it's easier.'

One of Ontario's last working tanneries supplies the hides. Ken slips one onto the machine and carefully positions a die, which looks like a glove-shaped cookie cutter. He swings the arm over it and taps a button; the arm comes down invisibly fast—Bang! Rumble. Next the glove halves are sewn together, inside out. Ken's brother, who also works at Dotzert, turns the gloves right-side out, finger by finger, using a turning tool. Then they are finished and shaped on ancient steam-heated, hand-shaped metal forms.

Ken started at Dotzert Glove when he was practically a kid. He has cut gloves for more than thirty-five years, but also has done sewing, turning and finishing. He says training someone to cut is difficult: 'You can't just say "This is how you do it," because each piece of leather, the grain could be different.... If you cut it the wrong way, it could end up stretching.'

The gloves Ken makes may be more expensive than imported ones, but he says, 'You get what you pay for.'

Louis Pfeifer, Shoemaker

Oh yes, I did make shoes.... You shape the shoe exactly the way the feet are. The most interesting was a young man who came in asking if I would make a pair of boots: Paul McCartney's boots. He brought a picture, and I made them for him exactly the way he wanted them. He had them for fifteen years and he still talks about them.... I'm not doing that anymore ...

☞ It's difficult to find anyone who is doing that anymore. Louis Pfeifer, a shoemaker's son, is one of the last shoemakers working in the tri-cities. 'I don't see any coming,' says Louis. 'Quitting, yes. But coming? For years they're just closing down.'

Growing up in Slovenia, Louis had his education interrupted by the Second World War, but afterward managed to finish school and learn his trade. He also learned how to make orthopedic shoes for the war injured. 'The older guys, they were real shoemakers. They were trained in Europe, different places. But the younger people, they just don't have training.' Louis has training. In 1954 he came to Canada, and in the early '60s bought a well-established Kitchener shoe repair business. He works alongside his son, fixing shoes and anything else in leather.

Louis says, 'There are only two types of shoes: bad, and very good.' His Singer sewing machine is more than a century old and he runs it slowly, controlling every stitch, moving the shoe under the needle with precision. 'It's an art. Fixing shoes is not so simple. You have to know how to make them first, to see what's involved, to see how things are put together, to learn that first, before you know what's wrong,' says Louis. 'The more you know about any life, or any thing, the more you respect it.'

Liz Morgado, Tailor

She asked me if I knew how to sew, and I said 'No'—and that was not acceptable ...

🖝 For Liz Morgado, a simple question from her future mother-in-law grew into an apprenticeship at Bart and Maria's, her in-laws' storefront tailor shop. Liz now runs the business, and represents the third generation of tailors in the family, but it was her father-in-law's early encouragement that convinced her she had potential. 'When he said that I was good and that I should pursue it, I decided that's what I was going to do,' says Liz. But pursuing it meant many years of training to acquire a tailor's skills. 'You start very basic: a seamstress.'

First she sewed hems and learned how to use the different sewing machines until she could expertly sew a blind stitch and serge a seam, alter a pair of pants or put in a zipper. Learning dresses took a few years longer, men's suits longer still, 'taking in sides, creating vents, lowering a collar on a suit jacket and actually shortening the sleeve from the top, narrowing the shoulder, shortening the bottom of a jacket.... You can remodel the whole thing.' Liz can now hem jeans in four minutes, but precision work such as narrowing a jacket is time consuming, and she enjoys the challenge of getting it just right. 'I love to sew, but I love the people,' Liz says. 'When they leave happy, when they put it on and say, "Now it's meant for me," that's a good feeling.'

Like her in-laws Liz wants to share her knowledge, but potential tailors are as rare as well-made clothing. The growing scarcity of tailor shops, once ubiquitous from coast to coast, bears this out. 'It's a great profession. It's unfortunate that a lot of it's dying out, especially the quality that people expect from a tailor or seamstress, because it's hard to find somebody who knows what they're doing. But I don't think I'll ever stop. And if I can train somebody I would, gladly. I'd like to pass it on.'

Ludovika Berta, Furrier

My father was in the fur business.... I started in Europe when I was fifteen years old. I saw what my father is doing, how he is doing it. I watched him ...

☙ Ludovika Berta is the last furrier at Kaufman Furs—'Twenty eight and a half years I'm working here, exactly'—and likely the last furrier in Waterloo Region, although when she started at Kaufman there were others. She pulls back the lining of a mink coat she is restoring to show how it was made by 'letting out' the pelts: lengthening and narrowing them by slicing each one diagonally into strips, then offsetting the strips and sewing them back together with tiny stitches. 'It's work. Thousands of seams, and lots and lots of hand work.'

Ludovika re-tailors vintage fur coats and hats, and repairs damaged ones using pieces from trade-ins and remnants, carefully matching the fur type and colour. After sewing together two or more pieces using a specialized sewing machine, she 'blocks' the joined piece, tacking it to a table fur-side down and wetting the skins. This makes the seams invisible.

Ludovika's father was proud that she followed in his footsteps, especially because, she says, 'The female job is always finishing ... but I learned every year a little bit, slowly ... blocking, sewing, I cut the fur, everything, because I'm working here by myself, so if I like to continue my work I have to learn.' Her uncommon skill set covers the whole craft, and she is glad to have a place to put it into practice. 'It is most important for everybody to work together. I can say my boss is really good and understanding.... When you have a small business you are working together.'

People have worn fur throughout history, some for utility and some for luxury. But styles come and go, sensibilities change. Of the local trade, Ludovika observes, 'Who wants to work in the fur business now? Now we are the only one—because we are the best. [She laughs.] We are the best.'

Aden Bauman, Watchmaker

Time is going too fast.... I still remember who I sold my first two manual-wind watches to. And the first automatic watch that I ever sold—I still remember who that was ...

◆☞ Aden Bauman started fixing watches on his twenty-first birthday. When he closed his shop in Elmira after forty-six years in business, he took his tools, workbench and some display cases home to his basement, and continued working. His skills are still in demand and his customers are loyal. 'I'm doing a fair bit of repairs yet that people can't seem to find anybody to do,' he says. 'I get some antique watches. I've got a pocket watch a guy brought to me. His father had it and he thought he'd like to get it going.... The pocket watches are usually sentimental.' Aden also offers a few new watches for sale, but luxury timepieces have never impressed him. 'What they claim of these expensive watches ... they're not worth what they're trying to say they are. Look at the amount of watches you could buy for that kind of money.'

That practicality has served Aden well, and even though fewer people are wearing wristwatches these days, his formal training as a watchmaker is also serving him well, especially as he has become one of the last around. 'I went to Toronto to a school for handicapped boys. I wanted to be able to earn a living for myself, and I went down there and they had different options, so that's what I got into,' says Aden. 'I did all right. I survived, anyway.... I didn't want to go to the government for support. And I supported myself, and I got married and had two boys, and I supported them, too.'

Doné Katsorov, Barber

I'll tell you what makes a good barber: you have to like people ...

☞ Doné Katsorov, who goes by Danny the Barber, has been cutting hair and philosophizing in Galt for thirty years. 'Sometimes I do the listening, most times I do the talking,' he says. 'If you want me not to talk when I cut your hair, it's gonna cost you more!'

Danny began barbering at fourteen, in Macedonia. He first visited Galt in the 1950s. 'You couldn't even find ten feet available for rent,' he remembers. Years later he came back, set up shop and watched as the downtown struggled. But now he sees signs of life returning. 'I see a brighter future,' he says. 'Each generation has its trials and triumphs. I'm optimistic.' Optimistic and gregarious. Danny's storefront window displays personal mementos and messages to passers-by, including a written invitation to stop in for a chat. If you also want a haircut he can do that too, and 'if you behave' he can even give you a traditional shave.

Danny is a barber, not a hairstylist. 'You have to take a course to be a stylist,' he explains. 'A lot of blow-dryers, washing, shampoo, spray ... I didn't have the patience for that.'

The ceiling of Danny's shop is strung with colourful garlands of greeting cards he has received. Snapshots encircle the mirror. Clippings, photos, cartoons, mottoes, children's drawings, certificates and correspondence—mostly from customers—cover the walls.

Danny is an engaged citizen, and the price of a haircut includes a debate. 'My favourite topics here are sex, politics and religion. If you don't know anything about sex you're not going to be happy. If you don't know anything about religion you'll end up in the wrong place. And politics? Somebody's gonna take you for granted.' Shelves crammed with books fill a corner of the shop. 'We're born with a capacity to learn,' says Danny. 'Every person you meet is your teacher. Right now we are teaching each other. So there you are. What else you want to know...?'

Stan and Howard Budd, Budds Department Store

HOWARD: Our father and his brothers purchased a business called Davis Economic Store in 1926. They learned the business from the ground up. They had no formal education at all. They went to 'the school of hard knocks'—that's how they learned their trade.

STAN: They stayed together until they retired, from 1926 until the '80s.

HOWARD: And when we got old enough we came into the store after school and swept the floors and made boxes and ran for coffee. And as we got older we were allowed to sell on the floor. And then we got finished with university and school. Stan went to work for the Hudson's Bay Company, and I worked for the Robert Simpson Company. We learned some good, we learned some bad, and our family asked us to come back and get involved in the business ...

✎ Main floor, clothing and accessories; second floor, bed and bath. Reduced items are in the basement. At the back of the store, upstairs in Stan and Howie's office, the four founding brothers stand close together in a photo on the wall, looking resolute.

As an independent department store, Budds is rare enough, but Budds is also the last of the many Jewish-owned businesses that had opened in downtown Kitchener by the 1940s, helping to anchor a thriving commercial district.

Howard: 'We have two- and three-generation families that continue to shop in our store. And hardly a day goes by where somebody doesn't comment: "When I was a little girl, a little boy, my parents brought me into this store; my grandmother brought me into this store; I grew up in this store."'

Stan: 'We couldn't be here all these years if there wasn't something special that we offer these people. And if you know your customer, and you have a niche and service it properly, you can be successful today, even in these tough times.'

Howard: 'We went to the big stores and we worked there, we went to university—but the best teacher we ever had was our family.'

Stan: 'That's right.'

Blair Rody, Rubber Factory Manager

When it closed, I turned off the lights and closed the door ...

🕭 The day in 1992 when Uniroyal-Goodrich shuttered its million-square-foot tire factory near downtown Kitchener, Blair Rody oversaw the final shift. He was foreman of the rubber-mixing department, and says at its busiest the factory employed about 1,200 workers.

Not too long after the closure, a few former employees established a spin-off business in the same plant, restarting the mixing equipment and filling custom orders for rubber. Blair was hired to oversee the operation. That spin-off has grown from six workers mixing small batches to become North America's largest rubber mixer, AirBoss Rubber Compounding, with hundreds working around the clock.

'My employee number is "one"—I was the first one to come here to start up after Uniroyal closed,' says Blair, now a manager at AirBoss. 'When we started, they were taking out equipment: tire presses, tire-building machines, calenders, extruders....' Some of the old machinery that was left behind now makes up the only fully-manual production line remaining in the plant, and Blair trains new workers to use it. 'I'm basically the only one who knows how to operate it,' he says.

Canadian Consolidated Rubber built its Dominion Tire plant—the long central block of the AirBoss building—between 1912 and 1914, when rubber, furniture, clothing, felt and leather were just a few of the downtown manufacturing industries that surely must have seemed as permanent as the dozens of factory buildings that housed them. By the end of the century many of those industries and factories had disappeared, but Blair and his coworkers bucked the trend. 'The rubber is all gone now, except for this place here,' he says. 'If you would have asked me nineteen years ago if it would have gotten this big, I would have said "not likely". And here we are, twenty-four seven!'

Ronald Schaus, Rubber Worker

We would drive past here, and my mother would always say to my dad, 'Look at all the new cars sitting in the parking lot. They must make good money!' I always remember that ...

→ After driving past the giant Dominion Tire factory, young Ronald Schaus and his parents could have driven on, passing through downtown Kitchener, passing one busy factory after another. Some of those buildings remain today, but almost none are still engaged in manufacturing.

One exception is the Dominion plant Ron drove past as a kid, and where he started punching-in for work shifts in the early 1970s. 'My brother-in-law worked here. My father-in-law was here. So then I got in,' he recalls. It was Uniroyal by then, and Ron built tire treads. 'You were trained on the job. We did work for Sears, Esso, Shell. GM— we did an awful lot for GM. Every eight-hour shift it would be between 6,000, 7,000 treads.'

After coming off Ron's machine (tread tuber 3), the treads, along with tire parts made elsewhere in the factory, went upstairs where everything came together in the tire-building machines. Just before the factory closed in 1992, Ron saw that final stage of the process for the first time, and it made a lasting impression. 'You just couldn't understand it if you didn't see it. It would blow your mind.'

A few years later some former employees reopened the place as a custom rubber-mixing plant, operated today by AirBoss Rubber Compounding. Ron was hired back to run one of the rubber mills, which forms mixed rubber into continuous sheets. He has worked the same piece of vintage equipment ever since.

The rubber industry came to the region around 1900 and now has nearly gone, but Ron is a career rubber worker and will retire as one, putting in his last shifts on a busy factory floor. 'That's about all I did my whole life. I made a very good living.... The funny thing is, I don't know where the time goes to!'

Stewart Smith, Patternmaker

I started off wanting to be a sculptor ... with a giant workbench that ran on rails that allowed you to roll it out into your hundred-acre park and work out there under the shade of the trees ...

✍ Stewart Smith was a young New Hamburg woodcarver when he visited nearby metal foundries to investigate having some of his work cast in bronze. At Riverside Brass, Ervin Steinmann took the time to show the inquisitive artist how to make a casting pattern: a duplicate model of the desired casting, used to create a detailed cavity in a mould to be filled with molten metal. Soon Stewart was making both industrial and ornamental patterns for Riverside. 'The normal way of becoming a patternmaker is to do a seven-year apprenticeship,' he says. 'I did it my own way, and it's been a living since 1974.'

Today, automated equipment fabricates most casting patterns, but Stewart still hand-makes his in wood and tooling plastic; patterns for everything from fire-suppression-system components to Parliament Hill streetlamps. A beautiful pattern he recently designed for a Supreme Court of Canada elevator control panel had to match the heritage building and also meet current code and accessibility standards. Riverside Brass cast it in bronze.

'New Hamburg is a foundry town,' says Stewart. 'There were actually small foundries in most towns, but someone started up a steam tractor company here and I think that got that whole set of skills well entrenched.... For a town of 5,000 to have had three foundries and a fairly substantial pattern shop said something about the community and its base of skilled workers.' Stewart's own skilled work comes from forty years of experience. It flows from his head to his hands, taking shape in three dimensions. And it flows from an era when, as Stewart says, industrial workers in towns everywhere 'used to all troop together into the plant, and they would spend their days working there. That world seems to be fragmenting, and kind of dying away.'

George Kakousian, Foundryman

Sometimes I sit down and think: How did they make the Tutankhamun? How did they melt the gold? In a big pot?... I still can't figure it out...

⚜ George Kakousian started as a mould maker in a foundry in Lebanon before coming to Canada in 1965. Since then, small commercial foundries like his in Cambridge, where metalwork is turned out in short production runs, have nearly disappeared.

Most of George's business these days is in equestrian hardware. 'There were over a hundred different items that I produced,' he says. 'There is a place in Rhode Island, they make only buckles, all kinds of buckles. There is another place in Boston, they make hames. There is another place in, maybe, Texas—they make bits. I make everything!'

Incandescent molten brass is poured from the crucible at over 1,000 degrees Celsius into sand-filled moulds stacked on a turntable, and unlike at big foundries, every labour-intensive step—mould making, casting, cutting, finishing—is done by hand.

George has always worked with his two brothers. 'They were loyal to me,' he says. There once were twelve workers in the foundry, day and night, 'but nowadays,' says George, holding up a brass buckle, 'the guy goes to China and brings 10,000 of those. It's so cheap, cheaper than the material. I could buy "Made in China" hardware, sell it as scrap, and still make money. So my business has dropped over 90 percent.' Even so, he says his shop can still serve local industries. 'If a machine part breaks they could bring it over, within twenty-four hours I could make another one.'

George is unsure how much longer he can keep the family business running, but is sure he and his brothers will be the last to run it. 'I started something I wanted my kids to continue, but my son, he doesn't want to work with this dust,' he says. 'But I enjoy my work. If you gave me a choice of going on a holiday or to work here, I will take another shot.'

Michael Eiche, Wood Bender

This trade's gone back hundreds of years ...

☙ And steam wood-bending for bentwood furniture goes back at least a century at Krug Inc., where Michael Eiche began bending solid wood chair arms, backs and rails in his late teens. 'My dad used to work here, too,' he says.

A city block long, Krug is the last working factory in Kitchener's historic downtown manufacturing district. Fading letters spell out 'H. Krug Furniture Co. Limited' on the four-storey yellow-brick façade that looms beside train tracks and the 1897 Kitchener train station (Krug is older). All the other downtown factories—there once were dozens—have either been converted to other uses or demolished.

Deep in the basement of the building, high-pressure steam is piped from the boiler room into the wood-steaming chambers, called 'retorts'. Next, Michael bends the steam-saturated wood one piece at a time on the Rye bending machine, which applies 1,000 pounds of force. 'This is spring steel, and we got two hydraulic cylinders, and we got this jig made out of plywood lined with aluminum. And we'll take a part, we'll place it in the tray, we'll place it on the Rye, and it'll wrap the part around the jig.... Here I'm bending some 2451 back rails in red oak.' To preserve their shape the pieces are then dried on tall steam-heated stacked presses, which are about a hundred years old (the rest of the equipment is not much newer). The bent and dried pieces are finished upstairs, where chairs and tables are made.

The carefully selected wood comes from Krug's own lumber mill, and the species, grade, dimensions, saturation and deformation must all be taken into account to ensure the wood will bend, not break. 'I also have to watch the end grain,' says Michael, 'because I want to bend towards the heart of the wood.'

Recently, some of Krug's wood bending has been outsourced. 'I think I'll probably be the last person to work down here,' Michael says, 'but I still have a good twenty years left.'

Jim Hanna, Upholsterer

I can do it better ...

⋈ Jim Hanna says he thinks this whenever he removes worn-out upholstery from a chair or sofa and finds design flaws and shoddy workmanship. It happens often. In some cases, properly finished fabric, or solid wood instead of particleboard, or well-installed springs is all it would have taken to produce a decent piece of furniture. So Jim fixes whatever can be fixed, and then reupholsters—the right way. 'You revert back to the basics,' he says.

Jim has owned the same Cambridge upholstery shop since 1975. He does the upholstering himself, and employs a small, highly skilled staff that includes a furniture refinisher and a frame rebuilder. Together they can refurbish just about any piece of furniture that will fit through the shop door. 'There's not much we can't handle,' says Jim, adding, 'If I could find somebody who could refinish as well as Brian, I'd farm it out. If I could find somebody who could upholster as well as me, then I wouldn't do it.' The latter seems increasingly unlikely; few people are picking up the trade anymore. When Jim started there were at least four upholsterers in the same part of town. Now he is the only one. 'It was more popular thirty years ago than it is today,' he says. 'The hands-on, practical work is attracting fewer and fewer young people.'

Jim also designs and upholsters his own hardwood chair frames. 'That chair will last for a hundred years,' he predicts, offering one on the showroom floor for consideration. It's attractive, compact, solid and comfortable. Ideally, Jim says, the dimensions of a chair should fit the body of its user. When they match up, sitting places no strain on the back or legs, and standing up feels almost effortless. By combining that kind of fit with good materials, Jim says he can build someone's favourite chair. 'It's just that little bit that makes all the difference in the world.'

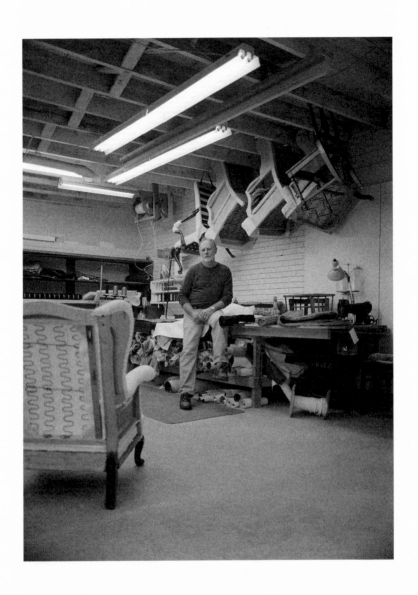

Joseph Bullas, Stained Glass Window Maker

Every step has to be followed religiously ...

⚥ There are dozens of steps involved in the making of a traditional painted-and-fired stained glass window, the evidence of which is everywhere at Bullas Glass, a circa-1950 building covered on the outside with brilliant yellow Vitrolite glass tiles.

Up in the second-floor studio, afternoon sun slants through window-mounted racks of glass samples, tinting the workroom a spectrum of colours. The shop, which once employed a crew of specialists—glass cutters and painters, window assemblers and installers—only survives today thanks to Joseph Bullas's complete mastery of the trade. Few stained glass studios still make large windows depicting human figures, so Joe is in demand.

Joe makes a typical window in about six weeks, from the first small sketches to the installation. After using a full-size drawn pattern to cut the coloured glass, he starts painting, and the blank material comes alive. He applies paint in layer upon layer, creating dimensional depth: saints' faces, draped garments, distant trees. 'You're painting with light,' he says. After each layer the glass pieces are kiln fired, irreversibly fusing paint to glass. 'That's why all the great windows in the cathedrals in Europe have stood the test of time.' Finally he assembles the window with lead, solder and cement, cleans it and it's ready to install.

In 1906 Joe's grandfather and great-uncle, glaziers and glass artists trained in England, relocated from Toronto to Berlin (Kitchener) to work on a big order for church windows. They stayed, and more than fifty years later Joe was making windows alongside his father, and also apprenticing in Toronto. He says the methods and tools of the trade have remained essentially the same for generations, but 'a lot of secrets have gone to the grave, especially when it came to different techniques. It's unfortunate, but that happened in so many trades. There were a lot of closely guarded secrets.'

Karen McLean, Mattress Maker

I'd been sewing since I was twelve, so I was looking for a sewing job …

✋ Karen McLean went to work as a mattress maker at Beam Bedding after the birth of her youngest daughter. Almost twenty years later Karen bought the business from the Beam family.

When she started out, she made spring mattresses and foam mattresses. Eventually she discontinued the spring mattresses. 'You can get that same comfort in foam,' she says, 'and such a variety in foam.'

Until 2006, when the last local tire factory shut down, she also had a contract to manufacture tire-tread liners. She says the extra work 'kept you afloat through the bad times. And that's a huge contract to try to replace…. We feel the pinch. It hit hard…. I can't even tell you how much that hurt, to lose that contract.' Rising material costs are another problem. 'When I took over the business, foam went up sixty percent, and it's gone up three times more.'

In addition to beds, Karen makes mattresses for boats, trailers and big trucks. Her customers like her work, she says, because she listens to them. 'People have got to stop buying with their eyes, and buy with their head.'

Karen once employed six, but now she and one employee manage to fill the orders. And because she would rather be busy with her hands than sitting at her desk, she is involved in every step, whether building a box spring, sewing a cover or cutting and layering foam. 'Everybody's a different size, different shape, so it's cut by hand, one at a time,' she says. 'I've always done it all.'

Lino Santarossa, Plasterer

I'm a social guy, I like to talk to everybody, so sometimes I get a little bit of pressure—they're pushing me to get the job done. But I always have a way to calm everybody down.... I don't get pushed around ...

✍ Whether he is creating custom plasterwork in a new house or meticulously restoring old plaster walls, Lino Santarossa does not get pushed too hard: plastering takes a lot of time, there is no room for sloppiness and few others in the building trades know how to make real plaster walls, ceilings and decorative mouldings anymore.

Lino and his thirteen siblings grew up on a farm in Italy. In the 1960s he visited Canada to see his brother, a plasterer, and Lino stayed and learned the trade himself.

Inside a half-completed custom home, Lino is moving nimbly across a work platform, smoothing the wet plaster of a ceiling with quick trowel strokes. In the next room, a curved two-storey plaster wall he trowelled six or seven times has just set; the rock-hard surface is flawlessly smooth, and cool to the touch, like marble. 'It's nice to work with people who understand the beauty of the job,' says Lino. 'Speed is not my priority. Don't give me twenty days to finish a house. I can't do that.'

Lino estimates there may be five trained plasterers still working locally, but says, 'We used to be 250 plasterers in this city. And then they came out with the drywall, so we could not keep up—the production of the houses was going too fast. They went with drywall, which is not the greatest. There's no finesse.'

When he is not plastering, Lino enjoys travelling, seeing great art and watching skilled manual workers. 'Not too many people know how to work with their hands anymore. We are running out. The young ones, they don't want to learn and get dirty like this. See, that's a problem,' he warns. 'It's a dying trade.'

John Davenport, Broom Maker

People still need a good broom. We're still selling lots of brooms …

❧ John Davenport bought the Irvin W. Hamel & Son broom works in 1989. 'It started back in 1908 … and it hasn't changed much.' John says there once were several corn-broom makers in the Kitchener-Waterloo area. Now he is the last. Most of the Canadian broom companies closed decades ago, he says, and he knows of no other manufacturers left in the country. 'All the brooms now are coming from Mexico, where the labour is a lot cheaper…. Basically that's why we're one of the last corn-broom shops left.'

John says his light-duty brooms are better than imported heavy-duty ones. 'We had a lady come back yesterday, said she finally had to come and get a new broom because it was about eight years ago she bought one and she needed another one.'

After a half-finished broom comes off the winding machine, where another worker wires broomcorn onto the hardwood handle, John sews the broom head flat using a purpose-built machine dated 1947. The machine clamps the head while he loops cord around it. Then, from one edge to the other in a single movement, the machine runs stitches through the broomcorn, catching the looped cord and binding the broom tightly.

Before John started at Hamel there were about six workers at a time in the shop. Now, he and one employee together make about a hundred brooms a day. They make a few different models, including a traditional curling broom. John sells mostly to stores, but he says being in St. Jacobs means he gets plenty of walk-in customers. 'We still make a half-decent living.'

Dave Pickering, Broom Winder

I like working on piecework. It's better than working at an hourly wage—you'll work your butt off and then you won't get paid a cent more if you're working by the hour. And I like to work hard so this is a good job for me ...

✒ There are five steps in the making of a corn broom, and Dave Pickering's job, building the broom, is step one. Dave winds broomcorn onto maple and ash handles at Irvin W. Hamel & Son.

He fits a handle into the chuck of an old winding machine, takes handfuls of broomcorn from the tub of warm water where it's been soaking, deftly layers it onto the handle and wires it down. 'There's five handfuls. And three of the handfuls get split.' When Dave finishes the brooms they go into a drying rack until the next day, when they will be scraped clean, sewn flat and trimmed. He works quickly with his tools—a broom hammer and two broom knives. It takes Dave three minutes to wind a broom, and his boss three minutes to finish it. 'I usually do about twenty an hour,' he says. The broomcorn, *Sorghum vulgare*, comes from North Carolina, the stiff cane used in the centre of Hamel's heavy-duty 1-W-1 model comes from India, and the handles come from Quebec.

Dave says that business has just recently slowed down a bit. 'Last year this time I was working five, six, sometimes even seven days a week. Now I'm down to four, sometimes even three.'

Stuart Trussler, Kitchener Farmer

I always wanted to be a farmer, follow in my dad's footsteps. I just enjoy working outside and working with animals. I like animals...

☙ On the barn where Trussler Road meets Huron Road, big letters spell out TRUSSLER FARMS SINCE 1841. Stuart Trussler and his brother are the fifth generation working this family farm. They grow wheat, corn and soybeans on about 300 acres. They also raise beef cattle: 'We used to have over 200,' Stuart says, 'but as I'm sixty-nine, I'm slowing down.' Stuart doesn't appear to be slowing down. His workday begins at five o'clock in the morning and usually ends after dark.

When Waterloo Region was created and its municipal boundaries were redrawn in 1973, a handful of farms, including Trussler, suddenly found themselves within Kitchener city limits. Those farms have been giving way to suburban development ever since then, and today few remain. 'Speculators have bought farms in close to the cities,' says Stuart. 'You don't have many neighbours like you did before—farming neighbours, I should say.' Farming practices have changed, too. 'Everything changes, but it's so gradual that you don't notice it,' he says. 'Used to be everybody had a mixed farm. They'd have some cows, some pigs and some chickens. Well, now there's dairy farms and there's poultry farms and there's beef farms....'

Stuart and his wife have five children and fourteen grandchildren, but he and his brother may be the last generation to work this farm. 'Time will tell,' he says, adding that he is not ready to retire. 'I look forward to getting up every morning and farming. There's people that work and just can't wait until Friday.'

Lynn Franklin, Seed Packer

I'm not a good gardener. I don't have the patience for it ...

⚓ Lynn Franklin may not plant seeds herself, but at the Ontario Seed Company one of her main jobs—which change with the seasons—is to pack thousands of envelopes and pouches with hundreds of seed varieties, all destined for gardens and farms across Canada.

Established in 1894, Ontario Seed is a fifth-generation family business where packing seeds has been done the same way for as long as anyone can remember—which is a very long time, considering that the employees tend to stick around. 'People stay,' says Lynn. 'A lot of them are here forever.'

Lynn has packed countless seeds during her thirty years with the company. The packing machines have served even longer. The Ballard, a machine almost as old as Ontario Seed itself, is sturdy and reliable; a good thing, considering it's also rare enough that any repairs must be performed in-house, and with a dash of improvisation. Today Lynn is packing seed corn on the Ballard.

The packing is choreographed to a steady rhythm, with several machines humming, clacking, moving all at once, and alongside each machine an operator closely tending it, working synchronously. This suits Lynn, who describes herself as having an 'old school' work ethic. It has seen her through a fifty-year career at a handful of venerable local companies: Electrohome, Beresford Box, Ontario Seed. 'I can't stand around doing nothing,' she says, already in motion as if to demonstrate. 'Give me something to keep me busy!'

Brian Bender, Feed Mixer

This is a scale above the mixer. The mixer is under the floor … and all of the various ingredients are brought to this scale, mostly via augers and gravity slides…. We work with a batch ticket, which is just like a recipe out of a cookbook…

🖝 Brian Bender is mixing another custom order for livestock feed at B-W Feed and Seed in New Hamburg. He weighs each ingredient on the scale before letting it drop into the mixer. Some of the feed ingredients are milled at B-W. Others come in from all over the globe. The finished feed goes out to customers across Southern Ontario. But Brian is a local guy, and B-W is a local business—one among the shifting number of small independent feed mills in the province. 'There are other mills—in Baden, but that one's closing. There's a thriving mill in Tavistock,' he says. 'Those would be the closest ones.'

There has been a mill on this site since the mid-1800s. In the basement of the current brick building, built as a water-powered flour mill in 1905, decommissioned turbines remain in place where water diverted from the Nith River once turned them.

Soon, to remain competitive, B-W will need to upgrade its equipment again, changing the way milling is done here.

Brian plans on retiring in a few years, and says, 'It would be difficult to interest most young people in this. It's hands-on, very manual labour, there's little to no computer work involved … and it's not really considered a trade so the wages would be correspondingly less…. As a part-time job while they're in high school, they haven't had any trouble finding kids—real good workers, but it's not something they'd want to stick with for life.' As for Brian, he enjoys his work. 'It's been a very good job, and it seemed like we could have a little fun, too…. And I think the business is solid. I think there's still a spot for this mill to service customers.'

Hilda Koch, Fall Fair Exhibitor

This may be my last year.... See, I didn't show much this year ...

🐦 Hilda Koch is at the 2011 Wellesley–North Easthope Fall Fair, looking over the more than fifty items she is exhibiting. 'As I'm eighty-five, I'm cutting down.'

The fall fair has been a part of life in Wellesley Township for over 150 years. Hilda has been going to the fair for about half of that time. Her baking and home-canned fruits and vegetables are prizewinners. In the 1930s, when she was still Hilda Hoffman, her baking earned a prized silver plate, donated by the T. Eaton Company. Seventy years later Eaton's is no more, but Hilda is still baking.

Hilda entered her first fall fair at the age of ten, competing in the public speaking contest. She didn't like it, so she branched out: 'I did writing—I had really good penmanship; I usually got good prizes for my penmanship,' says Hilda. 'And I baked.... I baked a lot!'

Annual fall agricultural fairs were first organized across Ontario in the mid-1800s, and were among the earliest-established community festivals. For exhibition and neighbourly competition, farmers and townsfolk went to the fair with the best from their fields, gardens and kitchens, as well as every sort of livestock.

The Wellesley–North Easthope fair is one of three remaining in Waterloo Region. Several others have dissolved or relocated. Attendance among exhibitors and fairgoers has been declining for decades, and Hilda says at one time farmers brought many more animals to show. 'I used to like to see that.... And years ago, on the fair night—which is tonight—they always had a dance in here, or the young people from the churches had plays.' Still, she is glad enough for today's fair. 'You can't be old-fashioned all your life,' she says.

Hilda is looking forward to the fireworks show later on, when the sun goes down. Afterwards she'll drive home in her 1983 Chevy sedan (which is in perfect condition). 'I'm still with it.'

Grace Pirie, Chalmers Presbyterian Church

It's amazing that at one time this church was filled. You know, you can hardly believe it.... That was before my time ...

❧ Grace Pirie's family connection to Chalmers Presbyterian Church in the village of Winterbourne began in the 1800s, when Scottish families settled in the area and established a congregation. 'From the size of the church, you can tell that there were quite a few people here,' she observes. 'It's amazing how there's so few Scottish people around here now.'

At many older churches in Ontario, especially small rural ones, membership has dwindled, weekly attendance is low and some congregations have folded, but at Chalmers a determined handful of individuals and families still gather in the nineteenth-century building for Sunday-morning worship. 'There's one that comes from St. Jacobs. The Conestogo church closed so they come here, that one family.'

Daylight floods the sanctuary through tall lancet windows. A stately-looking pump organ stands in a corner. 'We have an organist that comes up from the Waterloo Knox church,' Grace says. It's a few days after Easter, and fresh cut flowers scent the air. 'There was a baptism last Sunday,' she says, 'so there were extra people here.'

In Winterbourne the school and the store have closed, and although people still come to the serene village to settle down, 'they don't seem to be interested in the church,' says Grace. 'You hate to see it close, but it will have to.'

Jeff Stager, North Dumfries Township Farmer

We've got two types of farmland within the region. We have that group which is mostly the Mennonites. That is their lifestyle, and that will remain forever.... That's good. We're always going to have some farmers in the region. Then you've got the guys like us who are in the south of Wilmot, North Dumfries, parts of Woolwich—and we're just biding time. There's too much pressure from the city for expansion ...

☞ Jeff continues, 'The point is the price of land: up to $8,000 an acre. There is no farm, there is no agricultural activity whatsoever that can pay 8,000 bucks an acre.... Greenhouses, maybe. There's just no way you could site a viable farm here. The price of land is too high. It's way too high. You could never justify a hundred acres. There's no way you could grow enough crop. And it's come very close for me, because I'm at the end of my career....

'But here's the blessing of getting older: at the end of your life, you do have to let it all go. You are glad for the time you've had here, and you had a chance to look after things. This hundred acres here has housed me, raised me, provided my entertainment. This hundred acres of land here, how it grows each of the seasons.... This ground— some call it the romance of farming: the sun, a nice crop ... a calf dies or something fails and so on, but it's very natural. So I'm very connected to the farm. This property has provided for me. The sun shone, and the crops grew.'

Susan Douglas, Ayr Lawn Bowling Club

Really, the only thing you need to come lawn bowling is flat shoes, and you're in...

☞ Down a back lane called Tannery Street in the centre of Ayr, steps from the Nith River, Ayr Lawn Bowling Club secretary Susan Douglas is sitting by the close-cropped green. 'The club began here in 1895,' she says. It's easily one of the oldest institutions in this old town.

Lawn bowling clubs were among the first sporting associations in the region. Open to all, they have struggled to stay open: recently several venerable clubs have dissolved. The remaining few convene regularly to play, and take turns hosting tournaments.

A sign at the clubhouse door welcomes visitors. Inside, a young Elizabeth II shares the panelled walls with championship trophies from the past hundred years and vintage photographs of memorable tournaments and equally memorable floods—the low-lying grounds have been inundated repeatedly. Once, the rising Nith lifted the clubhouse clear off its footings, setting it adrift like a boat. After the water receded, holes were cut through the floor to let in the river next time.

'With lawn bowling, whoever shows up are the ones that play,' Susan says. Members range in age from around thirty to almost ninety; lately there were two eighty-seven-year-olds: 'They can just roll 'em! They were the best ones on the teams.' The bowls are biased, heavier on one side, allowing bowlers to send them curving one after the other across the green to the target ball, the 'jack'. By its nature the game breeds patience and good humour.

Dusk settles in. The early evening is warm and still. The river slides by tamely. Out on the green the opening rounds wrap up, and the lights come on. Laughter from the clubhouse porch plays back from the nineteenth-century buildings across the lane. Birds call from the riverbank. The bowls are taken up again. 'I hope that I'll be able to play for a long time yet,' Susan says. 'I hope there's lawn bowling in Ayr for another hundred years.'

Margaret Zoeller, Bloomingdale Women's Institute

We always felt that if you reach the woman, you educate a family ...

↩ Margaret Zoeller has been a Women's Institute member for more than sixty years. 'My mother and aunts and grandmother were all Women's Institute members.'

Through the Institutes, rural women in Ontario have lobbied governments, raised funds for charity, hosted educational talks and workshops and made friends. 'They were founded because the women never got to go anywhere. They went to church on Sunday, and that was it,' says Margaret. 'I was married in 1944 and moved to New Hamburg.... I was sort of a newcomer, and did not know the people, and especially did not really know the women of the community. And so it was really advantageous for me to go to a Women's Institute.'

After her home branch, Haysville, disbanded in 2006, Margaret joined Bloomingdale. The women meet monthly to work together on community projects and to socialize. 'The good thing about Women's Institute was the fact that some of these women you really would never have met. They would go to other churches, and had other interests. You probably would never have crossed paths with them, let alone become friends, and lifelong friends.... You hold those friendships forever—you really do.'

But much has changed for the Institutes. As more members began working outside their homes, they could spare less time for meetings. Margaret says the Institutes stopped catering local events, such as plowing matches. 'Now we're all too old and feeble.' [She laughs.] Today in Waterloo Region there are about a hundred Women's Institute members belonging to just a few branches. At one time there were dozens of branches and 1,000 members in the same geographical area. But at least one thing has remained constant, Margaret says: 'It's the joy of meeting people.'

Allan Fisher, Full-Service Gas Station Owner

I've been here since I was a kid …

❧ Allan Fisher is talking and fixing a tire in the service station his father, a trained mason, built with his hands in the village of St. Agatha. 'It was a crossroads,' he remembers, 'but there were three gas stations.' Now Fisher's Esso is St. Agatha's only gas station, and one of a diminishing number of small full-service stations in North America.

Allan started pumping gas and repairing cars here in his teens, and in 1979 he and his brother bought the business from their father. Even as the industry changed, they never considered converting to self-serve. 'Full service means we're gonna pump your gas, put air in your tires, check the oil, clean your windows,' Allan says. 'Most of our customers we know by name. It's that personal touch.' Some customers have been with Fisher's since the sixties. Some others switched to self-serve and saved a few cents.

The Fishers work twelve-hour days running the pumps, fixing engines, changing tires, shuttling customers home and back and talking with them (on the phone, over the counter, through car windows), usually about things other than their cars (village life, family news, church events). The brothers hire local kids to pump gas, training them to be polite and to look customers in the eye. But as for hiring another mechanic, Allan says, 'I haven't had an apprentice now for two years.' In fact, retirement is on his mind. 'Eventually we'll sell this place, and it'll get knocked down and it'll be turned into a convenience store, a pizza shop and a self-serve gas bar.' Soon after he offers this prediction, a woman who grew up in town and left years ago stops by to say hello, then drives off. 'I don't think I'll miss working on cars and getting cold hands all winter long, but I will miss the people,' says Allan. 'Somebody stops, looking for directions or wondering where somebody lives, or somebody's cat's missing. It's that involvement in the community that's part of having a business in a small town.'

Don Schnurr, Village Grocer

I just kind of inherited it, I guess …

❧ But Don Schnurr of Schnurr's Grocery in Linwood says he is not sure his son, who helps out at the store, will want to inherit the fourth-generation family business when Don retires.

Don's great-grandfather opened a store in Linwood in the 1850s when, he says, 'it was basically just a crossroads here in the middle of the bush.' The village is still small, but Schnurr's is busy. 'It's because of the horse-and-buggy Mennonites that we still have a thriving hardware store in town, and a grocery store, and a bank, and a feed mill and a couple of health services,' says Don. 'Don't get me wrong, the local town people do come in and support our store as well, just in a different manner. They come in and use this as a convenience store.'

Don says, 'If you drive through a small town in Ontario, you're lucky if you even see one store open anymore.… People drive into the big city to do all their shopping.'

In addition to serving a brisk walk-in trade, Schnurr's fills and delivers as many as twenty phone orders each day, mostly to local farms. Don knows his grocery is important to them. 'We just live across the street, so if there's a snowstorm in the winter, there's no excuse for me not getting into my store and opening it up. If there's power out—you know the blackout there, was it a couple of years ago now?—we just did everything on a notepad and calculator.'

Dieter Hiemer, Village Butcher

We're both here all the time. Dieter does all of the sausage making, and we both cut meat and serve customers ...

⫷ Sandra Hiemer is speaking for her husband, Dieter, who is more comfortable speaking in German than in English. They have owned St. Agatha Meat Market for twenty-five years, although the little shop opened in the 1950s. When they bought it, storefront butcher shops were common in villages and towns across Ontario, but regulations have become increasingly stringent. Most small operators have either renovated extensively or, faced with prohibitive costs and new reporting requirements, closed their doors. 'Three hundred butchers closed in Ontario,' says Sandra. But for now Dieter is still putting in overtime, working twelve hours a day, six or seven days a week. Each day has its tasks: cutting beef and pork for the display cases, or making sausage and cold cuts (Dieter's recipes are inspired by his Bavarian heritage), or preparing smoked meats (he operates one of the last commercial smokehouses in the region). By Friday, the display cases are filled with fresh and cured pork and beef ready for weekend dinners, barbecues and picnics.

Dieter and Sandra would like to carry on for a few more years and then sell the shop, but Sandra says it would be difficult for a new owner to obtain a licence for their kind of butchering and processing. 'I don't think they'd be allowed to continue,' she says, 'and without that licence you can't operate, you can't make sausage, you can't smoke anything, you can't cook anything. The way I understand it, once we're done here, that's it.'

Dieter says, 'It's too bad that all the little shops are going,' and Sandra adds, 'Everybody did their own little thing, their own recipes. They all tasted different. But now, it's the homogenization of food.'

Frederick Adu Lartey, Master Konditor

I'm always here anywhere between five and five-thirty every morning, except Sunday, when I don't work. And sometimes I leave close to seven p.m., so I have long hours ...

☞ Frederick Adu Lartey's workdays have begun before sunrise ever since he trained as a Konditor—a pastry chef—in Frankfurt. After a lengthy apprenticeship and master's certification, he applied from overseas for jobs in New York, Boston, Halifax and Kitchener. Over the years, he had met Canadian travellers who told him to go to Kitchener because of its large German-speaking population and so Frederick chose the Kitchener job at Café Mozart. 'All the guys working there came from Germany. So we knew what we were doing.' [He laughs.] 'We were busy, very busy.... We baked every day.' That was in the 1970s. 'The time goes fast,' he says.

After twelve years Frederick left Café Mozart to open Alpine Café, and found running his own business was different: 'You keep working until you can't do any more.... I work all the time until I get tired.'

As Waterloo Region's last wave of German-speaking immigrants has aged, many local businesses, including Café Mozart, have closed, and although he still speaks German with some customers, Frederick has been serving more and more people from diverse backgrounds. 'The business is a bit slower than it used to be, compared to the time I came here, but it's still okay,' he says, 'and the town has grown so big that I don't know most of the new places.' But if the town has changed, Frederick's insistence on only the best ingredients for his cakes, tortes and pastries has not—'I use real whipping cream, real butter....'—and occasionally he travels to Mississauga for specialty ingredients.

'The customers, they come; they don't go empty-handed,' he says. 'They always say, "Oh, I'm going to try this," then they buy, and they go. And they keep coming again!'

Erika Petersen, Erika's Bavarian Fashions

All year long we work for Oktoberfest ...

✒ Erika Petersen is sitting in the Kitchener shop where she makes, rents and sells traditional German costume for women and men. For thirty years she has outfitted dignitaries, dancers, musicians, pageant entrants and regular 'Oktoberfesters' who flock to Waterloo Region for the weeklong Oktoberfest, the second largest in the world.

Erika makes Dirndls and sends out extra work to another seamstress. Her sewing machine is stationed right next to the cash register. 'If I like the material I'll sit down, I'll cut out six, and I'll sew them in a week.' In the years when the pageant was held, she made the dresses. 'We sewed all their clothes for them.... Then they'd wear them for fifteen minutes, and I'd get the dresses back again: twenty dresses, all size six and eight—which never sell.' [She laughs.]

About Oktoberfest, Erika says, 'I've been in it from the beginning; first as a volunteer, then working in the clubs, then in the store.' Although Lithuanian-born, she got involved with the local German cultural clubs in their heyday. 'We had four big clubs: the Concordia, the Schwaben Club, the Transylvania Club and the Alpine Club. But we're getting older and the younger ones, they're not that much into it anymore.'

In the twentieth century, many Kitchener shops and restaurants reflected a large German-speaking population. Erika's Bavarian Fashions is now one of the last. At the moment, Erika is also the last tenant in the former K-W Labour Association building. The upper floors have sat vacant since 2011, and the other storefronts are in flux. But Erika's shop is cheerful, with every square inch put to use. 'We import tablecloths, glassware, beer steins....' Shelves, racks and walls overflow with souvenirs, gifts and folk costume in every size.

Erika hopes her lease will be renewed soon; she has no desire to move, or close. Each new day is interesting. 'Mostly people are very friendly,' she says, 'but there are a lot of shoplifters!'

Michael Fritsch, Fritsch Fragrances

It's the cheapest stuff I sell.... It's probably my best seller, too ...

🕮 Michael Fritsch is holding a bottle of 4711, the most famous of colognes. It comes from Cologne, Germany. Michael has never been there; he says he has taken only a few days off work: once for his own wedding, once for his daughter's wedding and twice for his parents' funerals.

Michael has worked out of the same King Street storefront in Kitchener since the 1940s. At that time it was Fahrner's Pharmacy, and he was the delivery boy. 'The city wasn't very big,' he says. 'You could get almost anywhere on a bike in half an hour at most.'

Later Michael went to pharmacy school, came back to work at Fahrner's and bought the business in 1959. He remodelled the place soon after. 'It was the brightest, smartest store in town. And there were a lot of people working downtown.... Everything was downtown ... jewellery stores, shoe stores, banks, clothing ... all concentrated in ten blocks at the most. So this is where the action was.'

The shop appears to have changed little since then, aside from the comprehensive selection of perfumes—the result of Michael's decision in the 1980s to move away from pharmacy and specialize in high-quality scents. But on the other side of his shop window, King Street certainly has changed, he says. He recalls how it got much quieter after the Fairview Park Mall was built, and yet by staying put for more than half a century, Michael has become a rare neighbourhood fixture.

He says his customers now are 'few and far between' and that most of them come in 'because they can't find what they want somewhere else', but their perseverance is not surprising to him. He has seen what a particular perfume can mean to someone. 'Women come in, and their mother, or their aunt, or their grandmother used to wear a fragrance, and they pick it up for her,' he says. 'Scent is a great memory.'

Delio Ribeiro, Corner Store Owner

I bought myself a job back in 1986 ...

🖝 That year Delio Ribeiro, laid off from his factory job, bought a vacant corner store at a quiet intersection in old Galt, fixed it up and opened for business. Since then, scores of similar stores have closed. Many that are still open sell little more than pop, snacks and smoking paraphernalia. Not Ribeiro's Market. Its two aisles are fully stocked with fresh bread and dairy and eggs, dried beans and pasta, canned vegetables, breakfast cereals, a bit of produce and yes, snacks and pop, too.

Delio says megastores that sell everything, including cut-rate groceries, have made it difficult for stores like his to survive. 'You've heard the one that says big fish eat little fish? That's the truth. The big fish eat the little fish. They still haven't caught me, though. Because I work hard. I work long hours, from five in the morning until six at night and seven days a week—on Sundays until three.'

The neighbourhood is residential and Delio is its eyes and ears. Delio's is one of those rare stores where regular customers linger to talk with the proprietor. 'They know exactly what time I'm here, so we can have a laugh,' he says. 'You always try to make them smile or laugh, because we're all just passing through. Never mind about what other problems you've got at home. When you come here, let's smile, let's have a laugh and maybe I can take that little bit of an edge off you.' Soon a regular comes in, buys a few groceries and jokes around before he leaves, chuckling. 'See? Now he's all fixed. Now he can go home,' says Delio.

Another customer chats with Delio in Portuguese and snaps a coin down on the counter to play an electronic lottery game, 'Wheel of Fortune.' He puts down another coin, then another. The multi-coloured wheel spins and stops; once, twice, again, missing the jackpot each time. They laugh. 'The wheel doesn't stop where it's supposed to,' Delio says, laughing. 'It's just like life!'

Mike Mihajlov, Small-Appliance Repairer

I used to take things apart to see why aren't they working, or why are they working, and I was always getting in trouble!

☞ As a kid, Mike Mihajlov stopped getting in trouble when he started fixing the appliances and electronics his curiosity compelled him to crack open. 'I guess I'm the one who takes after my grandfather. Back home in Europe he was the person in the village who repaired everything.' Mike started tinkering at age eleven, around the time his family moved to Canada. A few years later, working in a retail store, he found himself fixing the closed-circuit television security system. Next he added electric motors to his repertoire. Today he repairs small appliances, machines and electronic devices, even those generally considered impossible to fix or not worth the effort. 'I like to work on all kinds of different things, from a fifty-year-old Sunbeam toaster to a $30,000 medical laser.'

Mike can't think of anyone else in Kitchener-Waterloo who earns a living the way he does. 'There used to be one person, he'd been around for probably over forty years and he retired. So there's a lot of people that have a lot of appliances that they want repaired. They're not even aware that there's someone around that repairs these things.' If he can't find a replacement part, often Mike can refurbish the original part or recreate it from scratch. He says that some appliances, properly serviced, could work for a hundred years, while others are poorly made. And those that are sealed shut? 'I open them and I repair them! So many millions of dollars are being thrown out because people are not repairing them. Disposable. Where do you go from there?'

Sometimes Mike works overtime on something, free of charge, just to see it fixed. 'It is very satisfying when you find the cause. Sometimes the satisfaction is worth more than the money,' he says. 'I might be a little stubborn because what I've learned is that just when you're ready to give up, that's when you succeed.'

Steve Pond, Elmira Vacuum and Electrical

I had five days to decide, to run to the bank and see what the possibilities were. I didn't want to leave it. I didn't want to leave the customers high and dry, because there isn't another place around …

✍ When the owners of the electrical supply and vacuum cleaner store where Steve Pond worked decided to close, Steve bought it and kept it going. With so few vacuum stores still in business (it was once a more common type of specialty shop), the expertise and customer loyalty he had gained through the years seemed especially valuable.

That any vacuum shops remain at all attests to the repairability of these machines. 'A vacuum, you can fix it up, clean it out, get the air suction back to it again and off they go,' says Steve, adding that repair customers are 'happy that it's looked after and they don't have to throw it away and fill the landfills with it.'

Steve does the repairs himself. 'The oldest ones out there are the old 'Grandma's Electrolux'. They're tried and true, pretty durable little machines, and you can fix every part of it—motors, hoses, brush rolls, belts—and it still keeps going.' He also sells new vacs by Eureka and Electrolux, reliable brands with available replacement parts. He brings the same makes and models into the store over time, so he can get to know them and service them well. Steve says that parts for many other makes have become difficult to find in Canada. And some machines seem designed to defy repair. Steve calls these 'disposables'.

In addition to vacuums, the store also sells electrical supplies: switches, receptacles, wiring and lighting components. 'Every day is different,' says Steve. 'Every customer is a one-on-one customer. They come in, they ask a question for a belt, they ask a question for a switch and you go and walk them to the aisle, explain it and walk them to the counter. So I meet everybody and I help everybody, one-on-one.'

Nizar Govindji, Camera Store Owner

I used to work sixteen, seventeen, eighteen hours a day . . .

The toil of setting up his own camera store in the 1980s remains fresh in Nizar Govindji's memory, but he started down the path to proprietorship a decade earlier when he arrived in Canada with photographic skills that earned him good work, including a job at Toronto's legendary Silvano Colour Labs.

At Highland Camera, a faint telltale odour hangs in the air: film processing is still happening here. All camera shops once had this smell, but now Highland is one of the last that processes film in-house. Nizar says, 'We used to get a hundred rolls a day, and now we get only maybe five, or seven, or ten. The digital has gone quite high. But still, people don't print digital as before.'

In less than two decades, the photosensitive films and printing papers, as well as the chemicals, that constituted a hundred-year industry worldwide have been mostly replaced by digital technology. Now film occupies a specialty niche, mobile phones double as cameras and a 'photograph' rarely means a print, let alone a negative. Nearly all of the surviving shops have cast off their film-processing equipment and retooled as digital imaging centres and high-end camera sellers. 'Mostly the business is taken by big stores. Before, the people would go to the photography store,' Nizar says, 'but now they can buy these things everywhere at a cheaper price because they buy volume, and we can't buy volume. So, small businesses are dying for the last five years. About seven or eight stores, small like ours, all closed down in the Kitchener-Waterloo and Cambridge area. You have to change with the times, otherwise you are left behind.'

Nizar and his wife, Nusrat, work hard to keep the shop viable. Cameras line one wall, tripods and other equipment stand near the window, a section that displays frames also contains an in-house portrait studio. And, of course, they do a lot of digital imaging. Nizar says, 'This is the only way we have survived.'

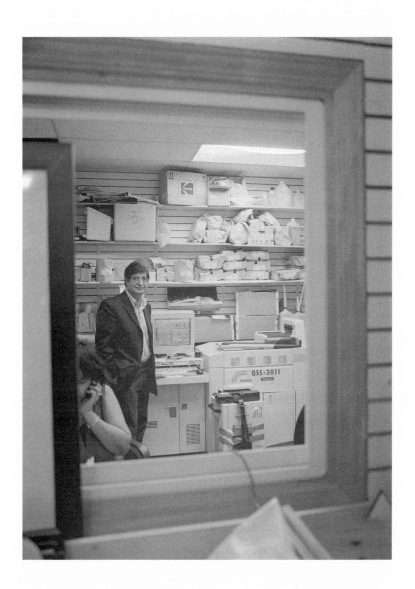

Manfred Aulich, Typewriter Mechanic

I will sell this machine…. Somebody's going to get lucky and get a really, really nice typewriter …

🐝 The subject of Manfred Aulich's appraisal is an Olivetti Lettera manual portable typewriter he recently acquired. Manfred says manual portables were still being made not too long ago and are sought after by writers travelling to remote places. A few reconditioned electronic typewriters are also set out on the bench in his workshop. 'Those are quite in demand. They're being used a lot by lawyers and people who do forms and certain applications where it's much quicker,' he says. 'But that's becoming less and less.' Manfred recalls other changes that have come along during his career, such as the IBM Selectric typewriter, a groundbreaker introduced in the 1960s. He retrieves a Selectric II from a shelf, plugs it in and types a line, its rotating type ball spinning in a blur of speed. 'Nothing could really come close,' he says.

Manfred has been working on typewriters ever since he trained as an office-machine technician in Berlin. 'We learned how to make parts. My apprenticeship was three and a half years. But we learned not just how to fix machines, we also learned fine mechanics.' Now he services many of the last typewriters in use in Southwestern Ontario and can fix any serviceable machine. He even takes emergency calls. When a local company that was having computer trouble phoned asking for a typewriter, delivered immediately, he says, 'I took this typewriter under my arm. I went up to the eighth floor. I put the machine down onto a table in the middle of fifty computers. And I got such a kick out of it!'

Manfred is also one of the last people around who services mechanical cheque writers and he can order new typewriters, which are still being manufactured. 'I can't believe I'm still doing typewriters,' he says. 'Everything is for a time in life, right? And typewriters had their time, and they still have some time left.'

Helmut Ostermann, Dictation Machine Dealer

I could rebuild one of those machines in an afternoon and have that thing running as perfectly as the day it came out of the box ...

☞ Helmut Ostermann is talking about a 1972 Philips magnetic-tape dictation machine, one of many he keeps on hand, ready to record. Helmut has been selling and repairing dictation machines since the 1970s. He says the machines he fixes could easily outlast brand-new digital recording devices, which he calls 'throw-away products', adding 'I just tell people, "When it breaks, please don't phone me." I can't do anything to fix the stuff.... You find the nearest garbage can.' A digital device is recording him as he says this.

Some law offices, medical offices and courthouses use dictation machines and some have kept their tape equipment rather than switching to digital. They depend on Helmut. 'I think I'm rapidly becoming one of the last people working on this stuff. I have a loyal following.'

Sitting at his impeccably tidy workbench, Helmut surveys a lineup of machines: next week's repair jobs. 'These are all out of courtrooms and they come from all over Ontario,' he says. 'I can basically tear them apart nut by nut and bolt by bolt, resistor and transistor. I routinely repair equipment that's thirty to forty years old.' According to Helmut, the 1960s in particular was a time of 'peak product quality' for dictation equipment. 'I never saw that kind of built quality again.' And he expects he never will. 'This old stuff had such a phenomenal lifespan. You're not going to find today's products delivering that kind of longevity. We're basically being trained to abandon that type of thinking.'

Rolf Glemser, Video Store Owner

There were only three rooms in my house that didn't have boxes of tapes in them: the bedroom, the bathroom and the kitchen ...

✍ Rolf Glemser started collecting videos in earnest in 1992 (he describes that early collection as 'heavy on the horror'). Ten years later he bought a downtown Kitchener storefront and filled it with his movie library, to rent, to sell and to expand with new stock, which he still brings in every week.

First the big chain video stores disappeared, then most of the independents. Now Rolf's shop is one of the last in the business.

Although not very old, Far Out Flicks is a classic. Through the front door and past the checkout counter are three aisles lined with shelves loaded with movies, floor-to-ceiling, in every category. 'There's a few stores in Toronto that probably have more than I do,' Rolf concedes. His dedication to hard copy makes the place a holdout from a time when music and movies were collected, curated and kept as tangible personal archives.

Within its own brief history, the shop has adapted to a technological shift from VHS to DVD and now faces another: the trend to watching video entertainment using no physical copy. 'I think people are tired of format changes, both in audio and video,' Rolf says. 'That mistrust is actually keeping VHS alive for me. We're still selling VHS, hundreds of them per month.... Two years ago we bought 12,900 VHS tapes off of a guy in London.' That collector was in the process of replacing his tapes with thousands of DVDs.

Despite all the changes, Rolf says his business likely has some good years ahead of it. In the meantime, he says the best part of the job is 'the homework: you take home a movie, you watch it and your homework's done!'

Kristen Hahn, Bookstore Owner

The most gratifying thing about what I do is when I match up the right book with the right person at the right time. It almost seems a little uncanny when someone doesn't know what they're looking for but you know what they need and that is an excellent moment; it's exciting, it charges me up and when they come back and tell me how much the book affected them, then it really feels like what I do is worthwhile...

☞ Kristen explains, 'Everything that I have in here is something I've chosen. I am the only filter here; it's not some corporate head office, it's not some sales team. You could go to a downtown in Winnipeg or Toronto or Halifax and see the exact same stores. It's the same thing over and over and over again. But I'm choosing books based on what my clientele reads. I know every single customer who comes in here and I know what they're reading and I know what they're interested in. I've watched their kids grow up; I sold them their first picture books and now they're teenagers....

'As far as how I stock the store, I'm aided by my publishing representatives—that itself is a dying trade. It happens twice a year that we'll sit down and do the orders. Like my relationship with my customers, my rep's relationship with me is similar: she knows what I stock. That's the difference of an independent bookstore. I look to the ones who are still strong; I think their undaunted enthusiasm is what keeps them going....

'I genuinely love what I do. I'm just really sad that it's becoming so difficult to do it, because I think that my role in this community, and culturally, is important. And it's not just me, it's all independent booksellers. We're finding it harder and harder and that's a shame. We're going to lose something crucial and we won't know how crucial it is until it's gone.'

Patrick Feaver, Bookbinder

From birth, to marriage, to death—all in one book!

☞ Many of the oversized, leather-bound family Bibles that Patrick Feaver rebinds and restores contain neatly handwritten pages recording a family's vital statistics over multiple generations. 'I find it fascinating. I look at the history: so-and-so got married, so-and-so had two kids, so-and-so died and it's all in that book. It's amazing.'

Lehmann Bookbinding is a family business in its fourth generation. Pat started there in 1961, learning the centuries-old trade on the job, from another bookbinder. 'I don't know a lot of the terms,' he says, 'I just know how to do it. And that's all that counts as far as I'm concerned.' Few other commercial binderies still offer Pat's kind of handwork in addition to their high-volume, production-line binding services. The small tools of an earlier era crowd his workbench.

When Pat rebinds a book, he saves and restores as much of the original as possible. He can repair and re-sew the pages, rebuild the spine, replace the endpapers, or make a new cover. 'Anything that doesn't work, I'll fix it.' He also binds and covers printed material for libraries, schools and religious institutions, embossing text on the covers and spines using gold foil, metal type and vintage equipment.

Pat has spent his entire career at Lehmann and still comes in to do binding by hand, he says, 'because no one else knows how to do it.' Meanwhile, after decades of steady work, fewer custom binding jobs have been coming his way. But to ensure that future customers have a place to bring their cherished books, he has been passing on his skills to a younger co-worker, because, he says, 'I don't think I'll be doing it too much longer.'

Joe Merlihan, Newspaper Publisher

The job market in '96 was not terrific …

✍ Joe Merlihan recalls the year he and his brother Pat, recent university graduates, chose to take their bleak employment prospects as a cue to start a weekly newspaper, *The Woolwich Observer*, in their hometown of Elmira. Pat had worked at a student-run paper; Joe took on sales because he had a business background, 'as much business background as you can have at twenty-three,' he concedes.

Launching a newspaper in a small market already served by another paper was risky. In the early days, cash flow was a persistent problem. 'I would have to go out and sell the ads, print the paper and then I'd have to go out and collect,' Joe says. 'So I'd go make the tear sheets, print the invoices and walk around and get the cheques.'

The Observer covers Woolwich and Wellesley townships and has a circulation of around 15,000. It's one of the very last independently owned and published newspapers in Waterloo Region and one of a dwindling number in Ontario.

Joe encourages his reporters, all journalism school graduates, to move on after a good run at *The Observer*. He says this keeps the content fresh while providing opportunities for emerging reporters. Opinion pieces are kept to a minimum and the Merlihans stay at arm's length from editorial decisions. 'All of it goes through the editor and he's very much aware that he's in control,' says Joe, 'and we don't always agree on everything that gets published!'

The brothers have been approached often to sell the paper. They are not interested, but do not think of themselves as holdouts. They say they simply enjoy the business too much to give it up. And Joe has seen too many papers come to unhappy ends. One colleague, who Joe says launched a weekly and then sold it to a big newspaper company, 'left six months after they started. The day you sign the papers they say, "Move aside, we're gonna show you how it's done." That paper no longer exists. It didn't even last a year.'

John Tutt, Cinema Owner

This projector here has got a patent plate on it: International Projector Corporation, 1939. And it's still working.... They just keep ticking ...

☞ John Tutt just keeps ticking, too. He owns two of the last independent cinemas in Waterloo Region: the Princess, a traditional single-screen art house and a newer, first-run cinema called the Princess Twin. John opened the Princess on September 18, 1985. 'The projectors arrived that day,' he recalls, 'and we projected *Casablanca* on mint projectors. It was unreal.'

As John threads a film through the rollers, he says, 'When we train new projectionists, this is something that we just go over and over. You need the right tension, you need to check your loops....' He switches on the machine and it comes alive, whirring and clacking.

It takes months to train a projectionist to take films from their cans and inspect them, splice them and build them onto the reels and then frame them, focus them and adjust the sound. John learned 35-mm projection at two Hamilton theatres: the Highland and the Broadway. 'We were projecting movies on twenty-minute reels, so every movie I had to thread up seven times. I got lots of practice.'

As digital technology takes over the industry, John will try to stick with film a while longer. But as for running his own movie theatre, he himself plans on sticking around. 'You're in it as a business, but you get such a kick out of it. The thrill of a busy night in the theatre can't be matched,' he says. 'It gets into your blood.'

Tedd Karabatsos, Film Projectionist

There used to be a lab in Toronto that would make all the prints for Ontario and that closed down and as far as I know we get our prints straight from Los Angeles now. They come in twenty-minute reels. I put it all together as one continuous big reel, which goes on a horizontal platter ...

⁊ Some of the last movies that will be released on film—the medium that dazzled the first movie theatre audiences—spool off big platters and feed through the old projectors Tedd Karabatsos runs at Kitchener's Frederick Twin Cinemas. He says, 'If something goes wrong I can pinpoint what the problem is, figure out if I can fix it myself, or if I can't, what part do I need to order to replace it.' As other theatres have scrapped their film projectors and installed digital equipment, parts have become easier to find.

Tedd is not sure when the last reels of film will screen at the Frederick. Likely very soon. 'I've certainly enjoyed running the projectors,' says Tedd, who learned on the job in London, Ottawa, Kingston, Windsor and Keswick. 'But here's the thing: I don't look at it in any nostalgic way. Technology changes. That's the way it happens, I'm sorry. It doesn't bother me that film is going. I mean, it bothers me in the sense that it's certainly a trade, something you learn that not many people know how to do, but we're still showing a film in front of a bunch of people. People love getting together and watching a movie.... Nothing compares to standing in the back of the theatre and seeing how people react. You laugh, you cry, all at the same time and that's a whole different experience from just watching it at home by yourself or with your family. Whether it's 35-mm films we're showing, or digital, nothing will replace this aspect of it. It's awesome just sitting in the back. Every single time, everyone's laughing at the same joke; you know it's coming and it's great. People laugh much louder in a theatre than they will at home. Because laughter is infectious, right?'

Joe Kelly, Town Clock Keeper

It actually is something beating inside this building, keeping it alive …

✐ The town clock in the tower of the former Elmira post office has ticked the seconds and struck the hours since 1914, even when the building has sat vacant. 'You had whistles to tell you when to go to work, you had whistles to tell you when to stop working,' says Joe Kelly. 'This clock told you when church was over—the church across the street—at twelve noon…. When this tower went off, the pastor had to quit his sermon!'

Once a week Joe climbs into the base of the tower to wind the giant original brass movement of the J. B. Joyce and Co. eight-day pendulum clock. Using 'elbow grease' and a two-handed crank, he spools up the weighted drive cables. As they unwind from the movement, turning the gears and striking the bell, the cables ascend two storeys, pass through a series of pulleys and disappear into a space behind the wall where they slowly drop. A gear shaft also rises two storeys to the uppermost room, where it moves the hands of the four glass-and-metal clock faces. In a room between the faces and the movement is the big bell. The clock loses two minutes between windings. Some locals tell Joe they set their own clocks by it.

Several tower clocks still operate in Waterloo Region, but Elmira's is one of the last in Ontario keeping time with a wind-up mechanism. Joe says it could run forever: 'The only thing stopping it would be somebody not caring.'

Most of what Joe knows about the clock he learned from its previous keeper, his father-in-law. Joe meticulously cleans and oils the gears; any debris could halt the entire works. He also makes repairs. 'You have to treat it like it's your own.'

The bell strikes eleven and the tower reverberates. Joe winds the bell, then the movement: sixty-four turns of the crank each. He is breathing quickly, smiling. 'We worry so much about tomorrow, but we should just live in today,' he says. 'Today is precious.'

Afterword: Faces in the Windows

☞ When I was little my mother toted me along on her errands around College Point, our neighbourhood in Queens, New York City. We called this 'going up the street'—the main street that ran from the north end, where we lived, straight through town and out into the unknown (actually, into a place called Flushing, where the subway connection with Manhattan begins, or ends, depending on your perspective). Almost everywhere in the city, most things were rundown, either a little bit or a lot. It was the 1970s.

Up the street, our destination was six or seven blocks of stores where some of the places were of a different sort than the rest—when we went into Empire Market or Zach's Bake Shop, Streich's Produce or Frank's Barber Shop, Katz's Menswear or Nelco Hardware; when on the way home we stopped at the candy store to sit on stools at the soda counter so my mom could read the newspaper and smoke while Bernie, the owner, stared out the window and I sipped a chocolate egg cream that was my reward for having not complained while my mom shopped; when we walked from our apartment to the old delicatessen-grocery, a place most locals called Schmidt's, some called Smitty's and a few others called Duffy's, even though the proprietor was a no-nonsense woman everyone called Ceil whose surname was none of those; when every so often our family ate out at Flessel's, College Point's creaky nineteenth-century hotel tavern; when I moved through these haunts I soaked up the strange atmosphere that hangs around wherever old places and old customs combine.

These didn't look or sound like the rest of the '70s I saw on TV, heard on the radio, talked about in the street. Something about them seemed permanent, the inlaid design of the neighbourhood over which everything else came and went. Ultimately, they weren't; only tough and fortunate. And yet when a place that had survived for generations reached an end, it was unsettling. Why was that? In my teens I got an inside look.

The deli-grocery, Schmidt's-Smitty's-Duffy's-Ceil's, was now Dolly Brothers. Jack and Tom Dolly knew me by sight, not by name. They knew that I was a polite neighbourhood kid who didn't steal from their store and that my older brother had worked there for a short while. And that was good enough—one day in 1988 I walked in and got my first job, on the spot, just for asking.

The Dollys grew up in the shadow of the enormous Ruppert Brewery in Yorkville, Manhattan, 'before', as Jack said, the neighbourhood 'went ritzy'. Many of the buildings (not the brewery) remain, but of the scrappy neighbourhood he had known, Jack said, 'There's nothin' left.' The brothers learned the grocery business young and set up shop successively in different parts of the city. By the time I worked for them, Jack and Tom were in the home stretch of a career behind the counter, and little neighbourhood stores well-stocked with good food and provisions were becoming a picturesque memory.

Jack and Tom were honest, funny and a little rough around the edges, but when serving customers—most of whom were devoted regulars—they (Jack especially) revealed themselves to be a particular kind of holdout: the gentleman proprietor. Deferential, but proud; familiar, but respectful; quick, but careful. To regulars who needed to eat now and pay later, the Dollys extended credit, interest-free, and they were discreet about it.

Jack teased the kids he employed that he was willing to perform any task at all in the store—which he did, perhaps chiefly to put us to shame. He worked in a white bib apron and tucked a pencil stub above his ear; if the cash register was busy he'd touch the pencil point to his tongue and tally a customer's grocery bill on a paper bag before neatly packing the items in the same bag.

He often referred to the business as 'nickel-and-dime'—it was no way to get rich and barely a way to get by; the hours were long and the worries constant. But he knew it backwards and forwards, and the genuine satisfaction he took in running a tidy, well-stocked shop was infectious. I worked four years at the deli and enjoyed the best times I've ever had at work.

ꝏ When I got my hands on the book *Harvey Wang's New York* it was my first day on the job at the Museum of the City of New York gift shop. It was the 1990s.

I was a university student looking for part-time work. I was captivated by urban history generally, and that of my city especially, so I registered for all of the related courses that I could. I was fairly ignorant but enthusiastic and had been thinking about potential jobs that might indulge my interest. Walking into the museum gift shop one afternoon I looked around and then asked the manager, Ann, if help was wanted. It was, and after a brief chat I was hired. I started the next day.

On my lunch break I browsed the shelves. Ann's guiding principle was 'more is more', and merchandise, mainly books, packed the room, with just enough space to move freely in between. There were perhaps 200 book titles, each examining New York from a slightly different angle. One little book had a black-and-white cover photograph of a typesetter gazing out at me from a newspaper composing room. I assumed it was a historical photo, but, skimming a few pages, found it had been taken in the past ten years. I forgot about lunch and stood there for the next forty-five minutes immersed in *Harvey Wang's New York*. The book contained fifty portraits of New Yorkers who, in their trades, professions or other activities, were among the last of their kind. The photos were straightforward, taken on-site all around the city in the late 1980s. Alongside each, a brief, evocative text, written by the photographer Wang, painted an accompanying portrait in words. I bought two copies.

The book was about perpetual change and quiet persistence. It seemed tailored to a particular interest I'd had since buying a camera and setting up a home darkroom: photographers of the 'disappearing'. Berenice Abbott, Irving Penn, Eugène Atget, August Sander and others had shown me vanishing New York, London, Paris and beyond. Now in *Harvey Wang's New York*, my fascination returned home.

A few years later I was a soon-to-be landed immigrant living in Toronto with my soon-to-be wife. I couldn't yet work, so I volunteered and passed time by walking the city. I roamed, surprised to see so many storefronts and businesses of the kind that had gone from New York; the kind Harvey Wang saw. When Jane and I moved to Kitchener-Waterloo in 1996, I saw more of the same. Years passed, but I kept tabs on the rare and quirky places.

✒ Toronto was changing, with neighbourhoods scaling up in rents, housing prices and building heights. Waterloo Region followed suit, fuelled in part by a tech boom. It was the 2000s.

Many twentieth-century places—downtown industries, little mom-and-pops—were quietly fading away. When my barber shut the doors of his eighty-year-old business I whined a bit to a friend, Sunshine Chen, handing him a copy of *Harvey Wang's New York*. I said someone should make something like it in Waterloo Region. He told me that, in fact, no one was going to make something like it and if I wanted it to happen I had to do it myself and stop whining. I agreed and cajoled him into joining me. The next day I resumed whining and procrastinating.

A few years later I read in the newspaper that the Rumpel Felt Company was calling it quits after more than a century in business, the latest in a string of similar closures. Finally, I phoned Sunshine and then David Rumpel, who was in no mood. But after I met with him he graciously consented and I arranged two profiles. We were hooked.

I compiled a wish list of disappearing trades, throwback businesses and rare cultural pursuits. I combed industrial directories and business listings. I drove and walked main and side streets, back alleys and country lanes. I made pop-in visits. The Fritsch Fragrances storefront on King Street in Kitchener had long been a favourite. Now I found myself standing on the sidewalk in front of the display window, shading my eyes to see inside. On the other side of the glass, Michael Fritsch's face peered back in mimicry, faintly grinning. I walked in and spent an hour booking our next profile. It was 2008.

And we kept at it, asking a thousand questions, exposing about as many frames of film, listening and looking, trying to hear and to see.

☞ In every generation things disappear, just as each of us has losses that are ours alone. Our lives, in part, are consigned to the past, but also are created each day in the now.

Back in New York almost none of my haunts still exist and only a few of the people. I too moved on. Even so, when I find someone from the old neighbourhood, the shop windows are fleshed out again, the small loss filled by shared memory.

But this book is not a requiem. Maybe a doxology for the unsung who get by, in every age, by unassumingly pressing on. Material obsolescence is no match for human endurance. Meanwhile, we'll often say something is a 'lost art' yet at the same time it's staring us in the face, found.

So, lost or found? Both, in perpetuity. We are most truly what we are when we are the sum of all we have now and all we have lost, one completing the other like two halves of a charm. And as for what we have now? Take a walk through town—my town, your town—and if your head is up and your eyes, then in the streets and in the windows, here and there, you can see holdouts of the future gazing back, and see all is as it ever was, and ever shall be, world without end.

Acknowledgements

We leaned heavily on many.

Karl thanks Harvey Wang whose *Harvey Wang's New York* was the model for *Overtime*; Sunshine Chen who advised me to stop whining and do it and then joined me in the doing; Jane Snyder for her support and our boys for their forbearance; John Woo who, while we were still in high school, showed me how a camera and a darkroom work and reminded me not to worry, but to try again.

Sunshine thanks Karl for accepting the challenge to take on this project, for the great car rides and chats on our way to and from the visits, for the opportunity to meet and talk to these amazing, interesting men and women who made it their lives to do their part and make Waterloo Region the place that it is.

We both thank the people profiled in *Overtime*, who freely gave their time and trust, who contributed ideas and leads and who each taught us a crash course in endurance; the people we profiled who are not represented in this book, and whose absence speaks only to space contraints; David Rumpel who got us rolling in 2008 when he let us into his factory; Tim and Elke Inkster at the Porcupine's Quill for making beautiful books and for presenting our project beautifully; Stephanie Small and Chandra Wohleber at the Porcupine's Quill; Steve Izma for his advocacy and enthusiasm; Andrew Savery-Whiteway and Eric Zeiburlins at Toronto Image Works for their skill and professionalism; Nora Young at CBC Radio for her generous spirit and for contributing her curiosity, knowledge and insight.

We are grateful to the Waterloo Regional Heritage Foundation for financial assistance in preparing the images for this book.

We thank those who offered leads, advice, information, interviews, encouragement, venues for exhibitions and talks and all kinds of practical assistance:

Marion Roes; Senta Ross; Russel Snyder-Penner; Konrad Sauer; David Antscherl; Tom Reitz, James Jensen, Kimberly Louagie and Kevin Thomas at the Waterloo Region Museum; Karen VandenBrink and Jinni Hartmann at the City of Waterloo Museum; Mark Connolly and Robert Barlow-Busch at Fluxible: Canada's UX Festival; the team at CBC Radio's Spark; CBC Kitchener-Waterloo; Doug Snyder; Peter Etril Snyder; Bill Kessler; Stephanie Walker; Elinor Rau; Susan Burke; rych mills; Margaret Nally; Barbara Aggerholm and Peter Lee at the *Waterloo Region Record*; Susan Saunders Mavor and Jane Britton at the University of Waterloo Library; Cheryl York and Carrie Kozlowski at the City of Kitchener; Laura Aivaliotis and Kayleigh Platz at Communitech; Jon Rohr and Paul Knowles at *Exchange* magazine; Bethel Lutheran Church, Kitchener; Steve Barefoot at AirBoss Rubber Compounding; Ervin Steinmann at Riverside Brass; Rick Droppo at Canadian-Made Apparel; Dave Bender at B-W Feed and Seed; Dave Dunn at Kaufman Furs; Brenda and Dennis Halk at Dotzert Glove Co.; Don Dotzert; Rob Lehmann at Lehmann Bookbinding; Carey Shantz at Krug Inc.; Clare Martin at Ontario Seed Co.; Stephanie Snyder at Waterloo 4-H Association; Mary Lichty-Neeb at the Wellesley–North Easthope Fall Fair; Ken McRae, Gail Michiels, and Susanne Gillow at the Ayr Lawn Bowling Club; Wendy and Ron Cascaden; Lary Turner; Del Gingrich; Nusrat Govindji; Julie Schnurr; Jenny Matthews; Gary Peysar; Gary Hounsell; Nicholas Rees; Kae Elgie at Architectural Conservancy Ontario; Susan Cook-Scheerer at Rogers TV; Stephen Jones; Linda Whittaker; Brian Douglas; Darin White; David Shaftoe; Jean Haalboom; Paul Tiessen; Marlene Epp; Pamela Mulloy; Cathy Farwell; Stefan Rose; Erin Bow; Christa Webster; Mirko Petricevic; Lynn Osborne-Way; Jennifer Cooper; Ann Goldsmith; Chris Cabena, David Worsley and Mandy Brouse at Words Worth Books; Mark Brubacher and Keith Kuepfer at St. Jacobs Printery; Karl Griffiths-Fulton; Mark Walton and the photographers of Foto:RE.

KARL KESSLER moved to Canada in 1996 from his native New York City. He works as a researcher and writer in the heritage field, and since 2003 he and his wife, Jane, have coordinated the annual architecture and heritage event Doors Open Waterloo Region. Karl thinks about buildings a lot, and how we can take the measure of a building beyond the usual (architectural style, historical period, technical specifications) to consider how it affects our thinking, physiology and behaviour, for the better or the worse. Other preoccupations include cultural change, our instinct for persistence and talent for adaptation, the nature of nostalgia, the meaning of work and ordinariness of creativity. And coffee with friends Saturday and Monday mornings. Film-and-darkroom photography has been a pursuit since his teens. He lives in Waterloo, Ontario.

SUNSHINE CHEN grew up in Waterloo, Ontario, and trained in architecture at the University of Waterloo. After graduating, he worked for the City of Waterloo in the planning, development and design of the city centre. He went on to start Storybuilders Inc., using photography, video and audio to tell the stories of people, places and organizations across Canada. Whether it's an oil sands heavy-equipment operator in Fort McMurray, a rancher in Saskatchewan, a tech CEO in Waterloo, a social innovator in Calgary or an Indigenous leader in Vancouver, Sunshine is interested in connecting people with their own stories, and understanding how big stories about community, business and society emerge from the richness and diversity of individual experiences. He recently moved from Kitchener-Waterloo to be a mountain dweller in Canmore, Alberta.

NORA YOUNG is the host and creator of *Spark*, CBC's national radio show and podcast about technology and culture. She was the founding host of CBC Radio's *Definitely Not the Opera*, where she often focused on new media and technology. As a journalist, author and speaker, Nora explores how new technology shapes the way we understand ourselves and the world around us. Her book, *The Virtual Self*, on the explosion of data about our behaviours, opinions and actions, is published by McClelland & Stewart. She has been an avid hobby podcaster since 2005. Her favourite technology is her bicycle.